FASTING

THE PRIVATE DISCIPLINE THAT BRINGS
PUBLIC REWARD

FASTING

THE PRIVATE DISCIPLINE that BRINGS
PUBLIC REWARD

Jentezen Franklin
FOREWORD BY TOMMY TENNEY

Published by Jentezen Franklin Ministries
Gainesville, GA.

FASTING
The Private Discipline that Brings Public Reward

ISBN: **0-9718254-9-1**

Published by Jentezen Franklin Ministries, Gainesville, GA.

For more information, contact Jentezen Franklin at:
Kingdom Connection, a ministry of Free Chapel
P.O. Box 315
Gainesville, GA 30503
888.888.3473
www.kingdom-connection.org
www.freechapel.org

All Scripture quoted is taken from the King James Version of the Bible unless otherwise noted. Other Scripture quotations are from: The Holy Bible, New King James Version (NKJV), © 1984 by Thomas Nelson, Inc.

The material contained in this book is provided for informational purposes only. It is not intended to diagnose, provide medical advice, or to take the place of medical advice and treatment from your personal physician. The author in no way claims to be a medical doctor. Readers are advised to consult qualified health professionals regarding fasting and/or treatment of their specific medical problems. Neither the publisher nor the author is responsible for any possible consequences from any person reading or following the information in this book. If readers are taking prescription medications, they should consult their physicians and not take themselves off medicines without the proper supervision of a physician.

Cover & Interior Design: Roark Creative, www.roarkcreative.com

DEDICATION

Affectionately dedicated to my deceased father,
Billy D. Franklin, my foundation, who shaped my life.

ACKNOWLEDGEMENTS

I wish to express my deepest appreciation to my wife, Cherise, for her constant support and encouragement, and to my dear children, Courteney, Caressa, Caroline, Connar & Drake…

To Dan Withum for his infusion of energy to get this book done…

To Susan Page for her tireless and wholehearted help…

To Tomi Kaiser for her ability to weave sermon stories and transcripts together to help make this book…

To my mother, Katie Franklin Lancaster, for modeling to me a fasting lifestyle…

To the Free Chapel congregation. Thanks for dreaming with me…

To the Kingdom Connection partners and friends for their support and prayers.

TABLE OF CONTENTS

FOREWORD

I count it a privilege to call Jentezen Franklin my friend publicly and privately. Many who minister have great public platforms, but not all of them have private discipline.

From years of friendship with Jentezen, I know there are certain times in the week when I can call his private line that connects to his private place where he's preparing for public ministry. I also know every January, I can call with my urgent prayer request, knowing he and his church will be on their 21-Day Annual Fast. I encourage you to read this book not just for what it will do for you publicly, but most of all privately.

TOMMY TENNEY

God Chasers Network

INTRODUCTION

What is the secret?

The question usually comes from someone with a genuine desire for deeper intimacy with the Lord and to know God's perfect will. For me, fasting has been the secret to obtaining open doors, miraculous provision, favor, and the tender touch of God upon my life. I was on a three-day fast when God called me to preach. I was on a 21-day fast when our ministry received its first million-dollar gift. When I was an evangelist, my brother and I traveled together. We would rotate our preaching nights. On my night off, I would fast all day for him. On his night off, he fasted all day for me. We went from obscurity to doors opening all over the world through the power of fasting. Every assignment has a birthplace. When God has placed a dream inside of you that only He can make possible, you need to fast and pray. Good or bad, what's in you will come out only when you fast and pray.

Now that I'm a pastor, our church begins each year with a 21-day fast. From those early years of ministry until this day, fasting has become a lifestyle. When I feel myself growing dry spiritually, when I don't sense that cutting-edge anointing or when I'm needful of a fresh encounter with God, fasting is the secret key that unlocks heaven's door and slams shut the gates of hell.

The discipline of fasting releases the anointing, the favor, and the blessing of God in the life of a Christian. As you read this book, I will show you the power of the three-fold cord. I will show you how every major Bible character fasted. I will teach you how to fast. Most importantly, as you read this book, you are going to develop a hunger to fast. I don't know about you, but there are some things that I desire more than food—"Blessed are they that hunger and thirst after righteousness for they shall be filled."

Since you are reading this book, you are probably not content to go through this year the way you went through last year. You know there's more. You know there is an assignment for your life. You know there are things that God desires to release in your life, and there is a genuine desperation for those things gripping your heart. It was for you, and those like you, that this book was written. Now I want to invite you to join this marvelous journey.

Jentezen Franklin

"Beware of practicing your righteousness before men to be noticed by them; otherwise you have no reward with your Father who is in heaven.

"So when you give to the poor, do not sound a trumpet before you, as the hypocrites do in the synagogues and in the streets, so that they may be honored by men. Truly I say to you, they have their reward in full. But when you give to the poor, do not let your left hand know what your right hand is doing, so that your giving will be in secret; and your Father who sees what is done in secret will reward you.

"When you pray, you are not to be like the hypocrites; for they love to stand and pray in the synagogues and on the street corners so that they may be seen by men. Truly I say to you, they have their reward in full. But you, when you pray, go into your inner room, close your door and pray to your Father who is in secret, and your Father who sees what is done in secret will reward you. And when you are praying, do not use meaningless repetition as the Gentiles do, for they suppose that they will be heard for their many words.

So do not be like them;

for your Father knows what you need before you ask Him.

Pray, then, in this way:

Our Father who is in heaven,

Hallowed be Your name.

Your kingdom come.

Your will be done,

On earth as it is in heaven.

Give us this day our daily bread.

And forgive us our debts,

as we also have forgiven our debtors.

And do not lead us into temptation,

but deliver us from evil.

For Yours is the kingdom and the power

and the glory forever.

Amen.

"For if you forgive others for their transgressions,
your heavenly Father will also forgive you.
But if you do not forgive others, then your Father
will not forgive your transgressions.

"Whenever you fast, do not put on a gloomy face as the hypocrites do, for they neglect their appearance so that they will be noticed by men when they are fasting. Truly I say to you, they have their reward in full. But you, when you fast, anoint your head and wash your face so that your fasting will not be noticed by men, but by your Father who is in secret; and your Father who sees what is done in secret will reward you."

MATTHEW 6:1-18 NASB

CHAPTER 1

FASTING FOR YOUR BREAKTHROUGH

As the deer pants for the water brooks,

So my soul pants for You, O God.

My soul thirsts for God, for the living God.

When shall I come and appear before God?

My tears have been my food day and night,

While they continually say to me,

"Where is your God?"

—KING DAVID [PSALM 42:1-3 NKJV]

W hat is fasting? Since there are so many misconceptions about it, I first want to clarify what fasting, Biblical fasting, is not. Fasting is not merely going without food for a period of time. That is starving – maybe even dieting – but fasting it is not. Nor is fasting something done only by a bunch of fanatics. I really want to drive that point home. Fasting is not to be done only by religious monks alone in a cave somewhere. The practice of fasting is not limited to ministers, or to special occasions.

❦

THREE DUTIES
OF EVERY
CHRISTIAN:
GIVING
PRAYING
FASTING

Stated simply, biblical fasting is refraining from food for a spiritual purpose. From the beginning, fasting has been a normal part of a relationship with God. As expressed by the impassioned plea of David in Psalm 42, fasting brings one into a deeper, more intimate, and powerful relationship with the Lord.

When you eliminate food from your diet for a number of days, your spirit becomes uncluttered by the things of this world and amazingly sensitive to the things of God. As David stated later in Psalm 42, "Deep calls unto deep." David was fasting. His hunger and thirst for God were greater than his natural desire for food. As a result, he reached a place where he could cry out from the depths of his spirit to the depths of God, even in the midst of his trial. Once you've experienced even a glimpse of that kind of intimacy with our God...our Father...the Holy Creator of the universe... and the countless rewards and blessings that follow, your whole perspective changes. You soon realize that fasting is an overlooked secret source of power.

> "A THREEFOLD CORD IS NOT QUICKLY BROKEN."
> -SOLOMON
> ECCL 4:12

During the years that Jesus walked this earth, He devoted time to teaching His disciples the principles of the Kingdom of God; principles that conflict with those of this world. In the Beatitudes, specifically in Matthew 6, Jesus provided the pattern by which each of us is to live as a child of God. That pattern addressed three specific duties of a Christian: Giving, Praying, and Fasting. Jesus said, "When you give"... "And when you pray"... "And when you fast." He made it clear that fasting, like giving and praying, was a normal part of Christian life. As much attention should be given to fasting as is given to giving and to praying.

Solomon, when writing the books of wisdom for Israel, made the point that a cord, or rope, braided with three strands is not easily broken (see Ecclesiastes 4:12). Likewise, when giving, praying, and fasting are practiced together in the life of a believer, it creates a type of threefold cord that is not easily broken. In fact, as I'll show you in a moment, Jesus took it even further saying, "Nothing shall be impossible!"

Could we be missing our greatest breakthroughs because we fail to fast? Remember the thirty-, sixty-, and hundredfold return Jesus spoke of (see Mark 4:8, 20)? Look at it this way: When you pray, you can release that thirtyfold return, but when both prayer and giving are part of your life, I believe that releases the sixtyfold blessing. But when all three—giving, praying, and fasting—are part of your life, that hundredfold return can be released!

If that's the case, you have to wonder what blessings are not being released...what answers to prayer are not getting through...what bondages are not being broken...because we fail to fast.

Matthew tells the story of a father who had a demon-possessed son. For years he watched helplessly as his son suffered with severe convulsions. As he grew older, the attacks became so severe that the boy would often throw himself into an open fire or a trench of water. A suicidal spirit tormented him constantly; the situation had become life-threatening.

Having exhausted every attempt to cure the boy—even taking him to the disciples with no avail—the father's plight seemed impossible. Then he heard that Jesus was near. Going to the Master, he cried, "Lord, have mercy on my son: for he is lunatic, and sore vexed: for ofttimes he falleth into the fire, and oft into the water. And I brought him to Thy disciples, and they could not cure him."

When the boy was brought to Jesus, the Bible says He "rebuked the devil; and he departed out of him: and the child was cured from that very hour." But what made the difference? After all, Matthew 10:1 records that Jesus had already given the disciples power to cast out evil spirits and to heal every disease. So why couldn't the disciples cast out the demon and cure the boy?

That's what they wanted to know, too, so later that night when they were alone with Jesus, they asked Him. Jesus replied, "Because of your unbelief: for verily I say unto you, If ye have faith as a grain of mustard seed, ye shall say unto this mountain, 'Remove hence to yonder place;' and it shall remove; and nothing shall be impossible unto you. Howbeit this kind goeth not out but by prayer and fasting" (see Matthew 17:14-20).

Now I've read that passage many times, and I've even taught from it on occasion. But each time I've focused on the statement, "and nothing shall be impossible to you." I think a lot of folks stop right there, but Jesus didn't because He knew there was more—much more.

See, that funny little word "howbeit" is the connection—it's the key that unlocks the power in the statement, "Nothing shall be impossible unto you." Jesus told the disciples they needed faith, even faith as small as a tiny seed. But that wasn't all. Long before this incident, the Holy Spirit led Jesus into the wilderness where He spent forty days and nights, taking no food. "Howbeit this kind goeth not out but by prayer and fasting." For Jesus, casting out that stubborn demon wasn't impossible.

> WHEN YOU FAITHFULLY FOLLOW THE THREE DUTIES OF A CHRISTIAN, GOD REWARDS YOU OPENLY.

If Jesus could have accomplished all He came to do without fasting, why would He fast? The Son of God fasted because He knew there were supernatural things that could be released only that way. How much more should fasting be a common practice in our lives?

Perhaps you're thinking, "I still don't know how fasting

can really be for me." According to the words of Jesus, it is the duty of every disciple, every believer, to fast. When addressing the Pharisees as to why His disciples did not fast, Jesus replied, "Can you make the friends of the bridegroom fast while the bridegroom is with them? But the days will come when the bridegroom will be taken away from them; then they will fast in those days" (Luke 5:34-35 NKJV).

Then they will fast. Jesus didn't expect His disciples to do something He hadn't done as well. Jesus fasted, and according to the words of Peter, Jesus is our example in all things (see 1 Peter 2:21).

"A disciple is not above his teacher, but everyone who is perfectly trained will be like his teacher" (Luke 6:40 NKJV).

There's another vital point that I want you to see in Matthew 6: God delights in rewards. Not only that, but He says that when giving, praying, and fasting are practiced in your life, He will "reward you openly."

A good example of such open reward can be found in Daniel. While in Babylonian captivity, his fasting—even partial fasting of certain foods—brought about the open reward of God, who blessed Daniel with wisdom beyond that of anyone else in that empire.

Later, in chapter 10, Daniel was grieved and burdened with the revelation he had received for Israel. He ate no choice breads or meats, and drank no wine for three weeks. Then he describes the angel that was sent to him—which had been *delayed* by the Prince of Persia for 21 days—with the answers Daniel sought. His fast broke the power of the delayer and released the angels of God so that God's purposes could be revealed and served.

This is just the tip of the iceberg. As you read on, I will show you how this threefold cord works in every area of your life. Do you desire to know God's will for your life, wonder who you should marry, or what you should do in a critical situation? I'll show you how fasting brings you to a place of being able to clearly hear God's will.

Fasting also causes God to target your children. You would be amazed at the testimonies we have heard about fasting. It also brings health and healing to your body, as well as financial prosperity and the blessings of God.

Whether you desire to be closer to God, or are in need of great breakthroughs in your life, remember that nothing shall be impossible to you. Fasting is truly a secret source of power!

CHAPTER 2

DETHRONING
KING STOMACH

Then Jesus,

being filled with the Holy Spirit,

returned from the Jordan and was

led by the Spirit into the wilderness,

being tempted for forty days

by the devil.

And in those days He ate nothing,

and afterward, when they had ended,

He was hungry.

—[LUKE 4:1-2 NKJV]

I f you are like others who have heard me speak on even a portion of what was covered in the first chapter, by now you are beginning to realize how crucial the practice of fasting is in the life of every believer. But as a part of that threefold cord of normal Christian duties, why is it so often overlooked? I believe the primary reason is one that has plagued mankind since the dawn of creation.

YOU WILL HAVE TO CHOOSE TO DETHRONE THAT "DICTATOR WITHIN"!

You see, fasting means crucifying what I refer to as "King Stomach." And in case you don't know who King Stomach is, just move this book out of the way, look down, and introduce yourself. You've probably already heard him rumble in disagreement a time or two since you began reading this book!

Every year our entire congregation at Free Chapel Worship Center participates in a 21-day fast. Without fail, folks share with me that they feel like eating everything in sight that last week or so before beginning the fast. But that's "ok." Once you make that decision to fast, even if it's just for a day, God sees the desire of your heart. He will provide you with the grace to endure and see the breakthroughs you need come to pass. However, you will have to choose to dethrone that "dictator within!"

It has been said that "the way to a man's heart is through his stomach." Most women have come to know it, but we need to realize that the devil knows it too! Some people—specifically Christians—could be the geographical location of the "bottomless pit!" Consider for just a moment what has happened to the human race while under the rule of King Stomach.

We can start at the beginning, all the way back in the Garden of Eden. The Bible records, "The LORD God planted a garden eastward in Eden, and there He put the man whom He had formed. And out of the ground the LORD God made every tree grow that is pleasant to the sight and good for food. The tree of life was also in the midst of the garden, and the tree of the knowledge of good and evil...And the LORD God commanded the man, saying, Of every tree of the garden you may freely eat; but of the tree of the knowledge of good and evil you shall not eat, for in the day that you eat of it you shall surely die" (Genesis 2:8-9, 16-17 NIV).

Seems straightforward enough, right? But the serpent was cunning and convinced Eve that she should eat from the forbidden tree, assuring her that she would not die. So when she saw that the tree was good for food...she took of its fruit and ate. She also gave to her husband with her, and he ate. (See Genesis 3).

And with that one meal, Adam and Eve immediately went from peacefully enjoying God's presence in the cool of the garden to fearfully hiding from His presence among the trees of the garden.

THEY ATE THEMSELVES OUT OF THE WILL OF GOD FOR THEIR LIVES.

They literally ate themselves out of house and home. They ate themselves out of the will of God for their lives. They ate themselves out of God's provision and plan for their lives, and out of His magnificent presence. But their stomachs were temporarily satisfied, and we still suffer the consequences of their appetites today.

When speaking of the sins of Sodom and Gomorrah, people usually focus on the rampant homosexuality in those cities. But that is not all the Bible teaches. The Lord said to Israel through the prophet Ezekiel, "Look, this was the iniquity of your sister Sodom: She and her daughter had pride, fullness of food, and abundance of idleness; neither did she strengthen the hand of the poor and needy. And they were haughty and committed abomination before Me; therefore I took them away as I saw fit" (Ezekiel 16:49-50 NKJV).

The first thing you may notice is that there was no giving

(poor and needy), and no praying (pride and idleness). But it is interesting to note that the inhabitants of those cities were not only guilty of homosexuality according to the account in Genesis, but as we see here, they were guilty of gluttony (fullness of food). Along with their other sins, their excessive loyalty to King Stomach carried them right into damnation!

Another brilliant example of one in whom King Stomach was high and lifted-up was Esau, the son of Isaac and Rebekah. As was the custom, Esau was endowed with the special birthright of the firstborn male child. That birthright brought with it his father's special blessing and certain privileges. It automatically insured that Esau would receive a double portion of all his father's estate. It was a blessing from God and not to be taken lightly.

Esau was a hunter. His father delighted in him because of the abundance of meat he brought to the table. But when Esau returned from the field one day, perhaps having had no success in the hunt, he was hungry. His brother, Jacob, was about to have a simple meal of red lentils and bread, so Esau, insisting he was famished and "about to die," begged Jacob for the same meal. When he impulsively agreed to exchange his birthright for it, "Jacob gave Esau bread and stew of lentils; then he ate and drank, arose, and went his way. Thus

Esau despised his birthright" (Genesis 25:34 NKJV).

Esau sold his coveted birthright because of his allegiance to King Stomach. God had a plan, a destiny, a will for Esau's life, but his lust for food and instant gratification were more important. The writer of Hebrews used strong terms to warn against becoming like Esau: "...lest anyone fall short of the grace of God...lest there be any fornicator or profane person like Esau, who for one morsel of food sold his birthright. For you know that afterward, when he wanted to inherit the blessing, he was rejected, for he found no place for repentance, though he sought it diligently with tears" (Heb 12:15-17 NKJV).

When God delivered the Israelites after 400 years of oppressive slavery in Egypt, millions of Israelites and a "mixed multitude" of others were miraculously led through the Red Sea on their way to the Promised Land. God provided for their every need on the journey, even feeding them bread from Heaven daily. This "manna" provided such a perfectly balanced diet that there was not one sick or feeble person among them for 40 years—with no doctors, drugstores, or hospitals. It filled their bellies and kept their bodies healthy and strong. However, "The mixed multitude who were among them yielded to intense craving; so the children of

Israel also wept again and said: 'Who will give us meat to eat? We remember the fish which we ate freely in Egypt, the cucumbers, the melons, the leeks, the onions, and the garlic; but now our whole being is dried up; there is nothing at all except this manna before our eyes'" (Numbers 11:4-7 NKJV).

God heard their murmuring and complaining. As any mom can attest, it is just not a good idea to get the cook mad at you. God said, "I will give you meat, and you shall eat. You shall eat, not one day, nor two days, nor five days, nor ten days, nor twenty days, but for a whole month, until it comes out of your nostrils and becomes loathsome to you, because you have despised the LORD..." (Num 11:18-20 NKJV). And He sent them quail in such a great abundance they stacked it two and a half feet deep! And they ate, and ate, and while the meat was in their mouth, thousands of them died and were buried there. And according to verse 34, that place became known as Kibroth Hattaavah, which means "The Graves of Lusters," as a memorial to those who ate themselves right out of the Promised Land.

The commentator Matthew Henry wrote, "But those that are under the power of a carnal mind will have their lusts fulfilled, though it be to the certain damage and ruin of their precious souls." I want you to understand that there are some "promised lands" and some "promises" that God has for you. In fact, we have an entire Book of Promises, but some of them will never be realized as long as King Stomach rules your appetites and controls your life. God had supernatural blessings to pour out on the Israelites in the wilderness, but they preferred their carnal appetites. Likewise, God wants to pour out supernatural blessings in our lives, but they will never be realized if we are not willing to seek Him in fasting and prayer.

GOD KNOWS THERE IS NEVER a "CONVENIENT" TIME TO FAST.

Are you ready for a "now word" from the Lord? Simply and directly He said to me, "There is never a 'good time' to fast!" That's right. God knows there is never a "convenient" time to fast. In our busy lives there is always a holiday, birthday, office lunch, or something that creates a bump in the road, so we talk ourselves out of beginning a fast. So my advice to you, based on personal experience, is to just jump in and do it and everything else will take care of itself! If you have never fasted before, just do it for one day and you will see what I mean.

The reason we fast corporately at Free Chapel at the beginning of every year is based on something else the Lord shared with me. He told me there were three reasons starting the year with a fast is a good practice. First, by doing so you set the course for the rest of the year. Just as beginning your day with prayer sets the course for the rest of the day and covers anything that may happen, the same is true of beginning the year with a fast. You set the course for the entire year by what you do with those first few days of each new year. You can carry that even further to give God the first part of every day, the first day of every week, the first portion of every dollar, and first consideration in every decision.

Secondly, the Lord said, "Blessings will happen for you and your family throughout the year because you fasted in January." Even in April, June, or August, even into November when you have Thanksgiving goodies on your mind, blessings will still be finding their way to you because of your sacrifice to the Lord at the beginning of the year. In fact, it was Thanksgiving Day when I got the call to go to the bank. When I arrived, a man and his wife met me and said, "Here is a million dollars for the building program." I had forgotten about the fast we had done ten months prior, but God hadn't. He not only sent someone to us with a million dollar gift, but also someone with a five hundred thousand dollar gift, a two hundred fifty thousand dollar gift, a fifty thousand dollar gift, and cumulative millions that came in regular gifts all in that same year.

This third point is so powerful. God told me, "When you fast at the beginning of the year and pray, you release the principle found in Matthew 6:33 – "Seek ye FIRST the Kingdom of GOD and His Righteousness and all these things shall be added unto you." If you seek Him first in the year, get ready for all these "things" to be added to your life throughout the rest of the year!

CHAPTER 3

HOW MUCH?
HOW LONG?
HOW HEALTHY?

I have not departed

from the commandment of His lips;

I have treasured the words

of His mouth

More than my necessary food.

—[JOB 23:12 NKJV]

In the last chapter, I described the downfall of some who failed to dethrone "King Stomach." But God's Word is full of marvelous testimonies of those who did. It was during a forty-day fast that Moses received the Ten Commandments (see Ex 34:27-28). When Haman ordered the annihilation and plunder of all Jews, Esther called for all the Jews of her city to join her on a three-day fast from all food and water. As a result, the Jews were spared, Haman's vile plan was exposed, and he was hanged on his own gallows! (See Esther 4-7). Hannah, greatly distressed over not being able to bear a child, "wept and did not eat," as recorded in 1 Samuel 1:7. God heard her plea and the prophet Samuel was soon born. Judah, Ezra, the people of Nineveh, Nehemiah, David, and Anna are also among those whose fasts are noted in the Word.

The Bible records many different circumstances, types, and lengths of fasts. In addition to those I just mentioned, Joshua fasted 40 days, Daniel partially fasted 21 days and often fasted one day at a time. It is recorded that the Apostle Paul was on at least two fasts, one for 3 days and one for 14 days. Peter fasted 3 days, and of course, we know that Jesus fasted 40 days in the wilderness.

The three types of fasts found in scripture are the

"absolute fast," the "normal fast," and the "partial fast." First, an "absolute fast" is extreme, and should be done only for very short periods of time. On an absolute fast, you take in nothing—no food, no water. Depending on your health, this fast should be attempted only with medical consultation and supervision.

On a "normal fast," you typically go without food of any kind for a certain number of days. You do drink water, and plenty of it! Depending on the length of the normal fast, you may also choose to take clear broth and juices in order to maintain your strength.

And then there is the "partial fast." A partial fast can be interpreted many ways. The way it cannot be interpreted is to include that time between about 11 p.m. and 6 a.m.—when you're sleeping! A partial fast usually involves giving up particular foods and drink for an extended period of time.

The most commonly used example of a partial fast is found in the book of Daniel. In the beginning of his captivity in Babylon, Daniel and three companions refused to eat the choice meats and sweets from the King's table, asking instead to have only vegetables and water. They did this for ten days to prove that they would be just as healthy as the

King's men. Later, in chapter 10, grieved over the plight of Israel, Daniel began another partial fast, taking no sweets, no meat, and no wine for three weeks, during which time he was focused in prayer. At the end, his prayer was answered by an angel.

The duration of fasts can vary. There are significant numbers we find in the Bible, which include 3 days, 7 days, 21 days, and 40 days. But there are also references to half-day fasts, and 24-hour fasts.

There is no real "formula" that I can give you to help you determine which type or length of fast is right for you. The length of time that you choose to fast should depend on your circumstances, but don't get bogged down in the details. Begin with one day from sun up to sun down. You will be amazed at the difference even a one-day partial or normal fast will make in your life. As a teenager, I would fast all day on Sunday until after church. It made me so much more sensitive to the Lord. I would be so spiritually "tuned in" that it didn't matter if anyone else got a blessing that day or not—I sure did!

Don't bite off more than you can handle. There is no need to be heroic and attempt a 40-day fast if you have never fasted a day in your life. Just start. Once you discover the benefits, you'll be on your way to making it a life-practice.

There are times when the Lord may impress you to go on a longer fast, but for most folks, a three-day fast is very practical. A "Daniel fast," eliminating meat, bread, and sweets for 21 days is a fast just about anyone can handle as well. Some may think eliminating only those three foods from your diet for three weeks is no big deal. But if it means something to you, it will mean something to God. After all, when was the last time angels were released to speak mysteries to you like the archangel Michael spoke to Daniel?

> IF IT DOESN'T MEAN ANYTHING TO YOU, IT WON'T MEAN ANYTHING TO GOD.

On longer fasts, I drink water, juice, and even broth when I feel I need a little extra strength. The local Chick-fil-A has grown so accustomed to our annual fasts at Free Chapel that they now readily strain their chicken noodle soup so we can buy just a cup of broth!

I want to give you a few tips on fasting that I believe you will find helpful. Whenever you begin a fast, remember, if it doesn't mean anything to you, it won't mean anything to God. Without being combined with prayer and the Word, fasting is little more than dieting. But I want you to realize something very important: Fasting itself is a continual prayer before God. There may be days when heaven opens and your heart is prompted to deep times of prayer. But there may be other days when your energy is sapped and you just cannot seem to focus in prayer at all. Don't condemn yourself. God sees your sacrifice. When you are fasting is not the time to sit in front of the TV. Why would you want to torture yourself with all those food ads anyway?

I can tell you from my own experience—it's just not a good idea! It is my normal routine to watch the news before going to bed. During the second week of my very first 21-day fast, Pizza Hut introduced their new Pan Pizza. Without fail, during the news every night at about 11:17 p.m., those steamy images of bubbling cheese, thick crust, rich tomato sauce, and various toppings would take center stage. They would lift a slice of pizza out of that deep pan and the cheese would just ooze down. I knew where I was going at the end of that fast! I would actually look forward to those commercials! One night I was dreaming that I was about to stuff one of those slices of Pan Pizza. That dream was so real I remember my

FASTING IS LIKE "spring cleaning" FOR YOUR BODY!

conscience screaming, "This isn't right! Don't do it…you've only got another week to go!" But I stuffed it in my mouth and chewed and chewed. It was so good! I woke up a few minutes later, quite startled to find nearly half my pillowcase stuffed in my mouth!

When you begin longer fasts, it is not a good idea to gorge yourself the days before. You should actually begin tapering off your food intake in preparation. Regardless of the length of your fast, when you begin, you should try to drink at least one gallon of purified water throughout the first day. I don't recommend tap water because of the impurities it can contain. Purified or distilled water flushes the toxins and the poison out of your system, which will help you get off to a good start. It also makes you feel full! Water is the faster's best friend, so continue to drink plenty throughout the fast.

When I go on a fast, I often get a headache the first day or two. I've had a lot of people tell me that the devil gave them a headache. But, more likely, it is simply your body getting rid of the toxins that have built up over a period of time. See, fasting is like "spring cleaning" for your body! It gives your whole digestive system a break, and medically speaking, that is very healthy. The headache generally felt while fasting is a sure indication that you should fast. If you experience a headache while fasting, it is a sign that you needed to fast. The headaches are the result of the impurities and poisons the body is burning for energy. After three days, the headaches usually disappear.

Whenever you fast for at least three days, your digestive system shuts down. I'll be honest with you, it is not always pleasant. Some feel sluggish, have headaches, can't sleep, and let's face it...you are going to get hungry! But I want to assure you that once you get through those first couple of days, if you will keep drinking plenty of water and juice, those toxins that poison your body will get flushed out and you will find what can only be described as a "sweet place" in the fast!

Seriously, when I've been on an extended fast, during the first few days as my body emptied itself of toxins, I saw no angels, I heard no "violins." In fact, I didn't feel much like focusing on prayer and the Word. But without fail, things soon clear up, and you find a deeper place in God where the rest just does not matter.

Solomon said, "That which has been is what will be, that which is done is what will be done, and there is nothing new under the sun" (Ecclesiastes 1:9 NKJV). Though men and women of God have fasted since ancient times, today we have many new books on the shelves touting the healthy physical benefits of the practice. Even the Greek physician Hippocrates (approximately 460-377 BC), known as the "father of modern medicine," whose concepts have influenced the development of medical practices for centuries, believed fasting was very healthy for the body.

In his book, *101 Reasons to Fast*, Pastor Bob Rodgers sites many statements from Hippocrates and others who discovered the many medical benefits fasting can have on the body. Fasting cleans your body. As you begin a fast, you will notice a sort of coating on your tongue for a few days. It is a sign the fast is helping your body eliminate toxins. Tests have proven the average American consumes and assimilates 4 lbs. of chemical preservatives, coloring, stabilizers, flavorings, and other additives each year. These build up in our bodies and cause illness and disease. Periodic fasts are necessary to flush out the poisons. Fasting gives your body time to heal itself. It relieves nervousness and tension and gives your digestive system a rest. Fasting lowers your blood pressure and can lower your cholesterol.

[[Bob Rodgers, *101 Reasons to Fast*, (Louisville, KY, 1995).]]

Don Colbert, M.D., is a medical doctor who has researched

and studied the body's need to rid itself of toxins which cause illness, disease, fatigue, and many other ailments. While I do not attempt to cover every medical aspect and benefit of fasting in this book, I would recommend his book, *Toxic Relief,* for specific medical guidelines for fasting. His chapter, "Finding Healing Through Fasting," is an excellent source of information and cautions. He says, "Fasting not only prevents sickness, if done correctly, fasting holds amazing healing benefits to those of us who suffer illness and disease. From colds and flu to heart disease, fasting is a mighty key to healing the body."

[[Don Colbert, MD (Lake Mary, FL: Siloam Press, 2003) 155.]]

Dr. Oda H. F. Birchinger, who supervised more than 70,000 fasts, stated, "Fasting is a royal road to healing, for anyone who agrees to take it, for recovery and regeneration of the body, mind, and spirit." He went on to say, "Fasting can heal and help rheumatism in the joints and muscles, diseases of the heart, circulation, blood vessels, stress-related exhaustion, skin diseases— including pimples and complexion problems, irregular menstrual cycles and hot flashes, disease of respiratory organs, allergies such as hay fever and other eye diseases."

[[Bob Rodgers, *101 Reasons to Fast*, (Louisville, KY, 1995).]]

To test the results of fasting on the human body, Dr.

Tanner, another medical doctor, decided at the age of 50 to fast 43 days without food. He did so under strict medical supervision. At the conclusion of the fast, he was much healthier. At age 60 he fasted 50 days, and in the middle of his fast, he said he saw the unspeakable glories of God. At age 77, Dr. Tanner fasted 53 days and among other things, his once thin, gray hair was replaced by new black hair! It was the same color that it was when he was a young man. What's more, Dr. Tanner lived to be 93 years old.

[[Bob Rodgers, *101 Reasons to Fast*, (Louisville, KY, 1995).]]

Fasting slows your aging process. Moses fasted often, including two forty-day fasts, and the Bible says in Deuteronomy 34:7, "Moses was 120 years old when he died and his eyes were not dim, nor his natural vigor abated." Doctor Tanner passed on some advice from his own experiences, stating, "When you fast, drink plenty of water." Water is the great flushing agent in fasting. One of the signs these toxins and poisons are being eliminated can be seen by the concentration of toxins in our urine. These toxins may be ten times higher than normal when you're fasting. The urine turns darker because the poison and the toxins that are locked into your body that cause all of the diseases that plague Americans because of their terrible diets, begin to be washed out. [[Bob Rodgers, *101 Reasons to Fast*, (Louisville, KY, 1995).]]

It is also proven that fasting sharpens your mental process, aids and improves your sight, hearing, taste, touch, smell, and all sense faculties. Fasting breaks the addiction to junk food. Fasting can break the power of an uncontrollable appetite. Some are bound by nicotine, alcohol, drugs, but fasting can help break those addictions. [[Bob Rodgers, *101 Reasons to Fast*, (Louisville, KY, 1995).]]

Each year I encourage all the members of Free Chapel to join us in our 21-day fast. If in 21 days you can be a new person, why go the rest of your life feeling sick, weak, over weight, and run-down? Why not take a radical step of faith? We have only one life to give to God—let's get control of our bodies and go for God with the best we have!

CHAPTER 4

EVERY ASSIGNMENT HAS A BIRTHPLACE

My sheep hear my voice,

and I know them,

and they follow me:

And I give unto them eternal life;

and they shall never perish,

neither shall any man

pluck them out of my hand.

—[JOHN 10:27-28]

I love the statement Jesus made in John 10:27: "My sheep *hear* my voice." That is how He created us. He speaks to us, and we are able to hear Him speaking. Do you want to hear the voice of the Creator? Do you want to know Jesus more deeply? Do you want to know the direction He desires you to take in life? I do.

As I was completing this book, I was beginning my fifth 21-day fast since entering the ministry. I began my first one when I was just seventeen years old. My parents were always godly examples when I was growing up, so even at that young age I was becoming aware that fasting was a part of being a true follower of Christ. If you are a parent reading this book, I want you to know that even children can begin to understand these concepts, and it is important that they learn them at a young age.

Prior to that first 21-day fast at the age of seventeen, I had completed shorter ones. In fact, it was during a three-day fast that God revealed His assignment for my life. I was praying and seeking His will. That is when He called me to preach.

Recently, the Lord shared something with me that I believe will help you as you desire to hear His voice and know His will. He said simply, "Every assignment has a birth place." Every assignment, every call of God, every direction from Him starts somewhere. God has specific assignments for your life. But how do you discover them? How will you hear His voice? How will you know His will for your life, His plans for you? Who should you marry? Where should you live? What job should you take? What mission field is calling your name?

The answer can be found in the appeal Paul made to the Romans: "Present your bodies a living sacrifice, holy, acceptable to God, which is your reasonable service." Remember the three Christian duties I covered in the first chapter? Giving, praying, and *fasting...*that is how you "present" your body to God as a "living" sacrifice. Fasting keeps you sensitive to His Spirit, enabling you to live holy. Paul went on to say, "And do not be conformed to this world, but be transformed by the renewing of your mind, *that you may prove what is that good and acceptable and perfect will of God"*

FASTING KEEPS YOU SENSITIVE TO HIS SPIRIT, ENABLING YOU TO LIVE HOLY

(Romans 12:1-2 NKJV).

I am convinced that we will never walk in the perfect will of God until we seek Him through fasting. When you present your body in this manner, you open yourself up to hear from God. You will prove or discover His good and perfect will for your life. Paul was fasting when God called him and shared the assignment for his life (see Acts 9:7-9). Peter was fasting on the rooftop when God gave him a new revelation and called him to take the Gospel to the Gentiles (see Acts 10). Fasting prepares the way for God to give you fresh revelation, fresh vision, and clear purpose.

In the book of Joel the Lord said, "And it shall come to pass afterward that I will pour out My Spirit on all flesh; your sons and your daughters shall prophesy, your old men shall dream dreams, your young men shall see visions..." (Joel 2:28-29 NKJV). God was going to pour out revival—*afterward*. He was revealing His will for His people—*afterward*. After what? After a fast. Israel was in sin and God was calling his people to fast in repentance as a people: "Blow the

> FASTING IS WHAT PREPARES YOU FOR A NEW ANOINTING

trumpet in Zion, consecrate a *fast*, call a sacred assembly..." (Joel 2:15 NKJV). His promise to them was to pour out revival and blessings on the land. I don't know about you, but I'm ready for those "afterward" seasons when God pours out revival, when our sons and daughters prophesy! What are we waiting for when we read scriptures like 2 Chronicles 7:14? Can you imagine if believers in America really took hold of this...if they humbled themselves (fasted) and prayed? God would heal our nation and send revival!

But if He is going to pour out new wine, our wineskins will have to change. Jesus said, "No one puts new wine into old wineskins; or else the new wine bursts the wineskins, the wine is spilled, and the wineskins are ruined. But new wine must be put into new wineskins" (Mark 2:22 NKJV). I had never seen the connection between fasting and the new wine before. But if you look at this passage, Jesus had just finished telling the Pharisees that His disciples would fast once He was gone. Fasting is what prepares you for a new anointing (see Mark 2:20). God can't put that kind of wine in old skins. If you want new wine, new miracles, new closeness, new intimacy with Him, then it's time to call a fast and shed that old skin for the new.

Fasting is a tremendous weapon and a source of power in the life of a believer. The blessings in my life are directly attributed to the fasting in my life. I am not the greatest preacher; I don't have the brilliant mind that some have, but God said He is no respecter of persons. When you honor and worship God by presenting your body as a living sacrifice through fasting, you too will know His assignments for your life.

Perhaps you are at a place of such desperation that you just cannot afford to miss God's will for your life. I have known people who were literally facing life or death situations. They were trapped, they were under pressure by circumstances, and they were under attack by the enemy. The only possible way to survive was to draw near to God—from whose hand no one can snatch you—to hear His voice, and to follow His plan.

Jehoshaphat, King of Judah, was in a similarly critical situation. He was a God-fearing King who found himself surrounded by a powerful enemy army. Annihilation was certain without the Lord's intervention. Scripture records that, "Jehoshaphat feared, and set himself to seek the LORD, and proclaimed a fast throughout all Judah. So Judah gathered together to ask help from the LORD; and from all the cities of Judah they came to seek the LORD...Now all Judah, with their little ones, their wives, and their children, stood before the LORD. (see 2 Chronicles 20:3-4,

13 NKJV).

All of Judah fasted, even the women and children. They desperately needed to know the Lord's plan to defeat this great enemy army. In the midst of that assembly of fasting people, God spoke to His people through a prophet, who encouraged them saying, "'Do not be afraid nor dismayed because of this great multitude, for the battle is not yours, but God's. You will not need to fight in this battle. Position yourselves, stand still and see the salvation of the LORD, who is with you, O Judah and Jerusalem! Do not fear or be dismayed; tomorrow go out against them, for the LORD is with you" (2 Chronicles 20:15,17).

In the midst of the whole assembly, God told Judah exactly how that enemy army would approach and exactly what they were to do in response. They gave tremendous praise to the Lord and He set ambushes against the enemy army and defeated them. None escaped. When the people of Judah arrived, it took them three whole days to carry away the spoil!

Do you want God to tell you what you need to do at this time in your life? Fast, worship, and seek Him. Be still and see the salvation of the Lord! They didn't even have to fight. God fought for them. The battle took one day, and God not only delivered them, He prospered them. It took them three days to carry off all the riches! I'm ready for some of those victories where it takes me longer to bring the victory home than it took to fight the battle! Press-in like Jehoshaphat in times of great distress — you and your whole family — perhaps even your entire church. God will deliver you and show you His plan!

Satan gets disturbed—and defeated—when you decide to do more than be a Sunday morning Christian. He has probably tried repeatedly to distract you from reading this chapter already. The devil knows fasting releases God's power.

Have you ever wondered why, of all things, Satan tempted Jesus at the end of His fast by provoking Him to turn stones into bread? Jesus had the power to do so, but He came to use His power to serve others, not Himself. Further, He was determined to complete the fast, God had called Him to finish. Jesus knew that some of the benefits of fasting cannot be released otherwise—and so did the devil! When Jesus returned from that 40-day fast, He immediately began to do mighty miracles, "healing all who were oppressed by the devil!" Satan needed to get Jesus focused on His appetite because if he didn't, Jesus was going to receive power from

God that would change the world!

Remember, the enemy's agenda is to steal, kill, and destroy you (see John 10:10). Do you think the enemy *wants* you to believe that nothing is impossible for you? He knows he is defeated, but he doesn't want you to know it or to walk in that realm of God's power. That is why it is so crucial for him to get you distracted. Don't allow the enemies in your life to cause you to focus more on your appetite or circumstances than on the promises of God that are released when you employ the powerful weapon of fasting.

CHAPTER 5

swatting flies

For you were once darkness,

but now you are light in the Lord.

Walk as children of light

(for the fruit of the Spirit is in all

goodness, righteousness, and truth),

finding out what is acceptable

to the Lord.

—PAUL [EPHEPHIANS 5:8-10 NKJV]

We begin each New Year at Free Chapel with a 21-day corporate fast. Everyone participates in some measure. Some may fast one day, others three days, some a week, some even the full 21 days. As a body, when we all fast together over that 21-day period, God is honored, and He rewards that sacrifice corporately and individually. But some people are never satisfied. I've had people testify that only *three days* into a fast for a loved one suffering with cancer—the cancer was completely cured! Another lady's son was dying from a 107 degree fever associated with his leukemia. The very first day of the fast, the boy's fever broke and he didn't suffer a trace of brain damage!

They both received miraculous rewards from God for their sacrifices. But that just was not enough. Both of them continued fasting for the 21 days. In fact, one of them went past the 21 days, and continued for a full 40 days. As you will see in the last chapter, her son's cancer not only went into remission, but the financial hindrances she had battled in her life were supernaturally broken.

Why weren't these people satisfied to fast just until they saw the breakthrough they needed in their lives? Fasting is not just a physical discipline; it can be a spiritual feast. Once you "taste and see that the Lord is good," your hunger for more of His presence eclipses the limitation of your understanding. God knows more about what you need than you do. All the fasts in the Bible—whether one day or 40 days—bring reward. But there is something very significant about the number 40 throughout scripture, especially as it applies to fasting.

A few years ago I was reading through a book someone gave me titled, *Prophetic Whisper*, by Richard Gazowsky. It is an interesting look at his journey to follow the Lord's call to build Christian TV networks. Early in the book he talks about an event that really got my attention.

Mr. Gazowsky and his wife were in a season of fasting, and were praying on a beach in California. His wife had apparently walked a little further down the beach and began praying for a woman they knew who was being tempted into adultery. The moment she spoke the woman's name out loud, "a swarm of flies ascended from the ocean surface, as if orchestrated by an invisible conductor, and swept like a blanket across the water and onto the beach." He rushed over to see if his wife was ok. When she told him she'd been praying for their friend, the Lord revealed what Gazowsky referred to as a "vulnerability in Satan's kingdom," that being the flies. [[Richard Gazowsky, *Prophetic Whisper*, (San Francisco, CA:

Christian WYSIWYG Filmworks, 1998) p 31-35.]]

When I read that, I immediately thought of the verse in Matthew 12:24, "Now when the Pharisees heard it they said, "This fellow does not cast out demons except by Beelzebub, the ruler of the demons" (NKJV). They were accusing Jesus of operating with the power of Satan, or as they called him, Beelzebub, which means, "lord of the flies." How interesting that, during prayer for someone being tempted by demons, a hoard of flies came out of nowhere and descended on this couple.

As Gazowsky found, the "weakness" relates to the life-span of flies. You can study just about any of the species and you'll find their reproductive cycles can range from a day to as many as 40 days. That is why, in order to exterminate an infestation of flies from a crop, for example, you have to spray pesticides for 40 consecutive days in order to utterly destroy them. If you stop short of the full 40 days, you will destroy only the existing generation, but the next generation will live on. Just as spraying pesticides for a full 40 days wipes out an infestation of flies, when we enter into a season of 40 days of fasting and prayer, we can break free of the bondages in our own lives, and into the

"...THE RULER
Of THIS WORLD
IS COMING,
AND HE HAS
NOTHING IN ME"

69

next generation. As Gazowsky noted, "The devil is a short-term skirmisher."

Jesus didn't fast 25 days, or even 38 days—"He was there in the wilderness 40 days, tempted by Satan, and was with the wild beasts; and the angels ministered to Him" (Mark 1:13 NKJV). Later, as time for Jesus to be crucified drew closer, He spoke directly to His disciples, sharing with them things that were to come. He said, "I will no longer talk much with you, for the ruler of this world is coming, and he has nothing in Me" (John 14:29-31 NKJV emphasis added). Satan was considered the "ruler of this world," having usurped Adam's authority. But he had nothing in Jesus...Jesus defeated him long before when He did not fall for any of the devil's temptations in the desert.

Some of you may have been battling with the same pesky sins, or worse, you may be trapped in bondages that you have tried to eradicate, only to have them come back time after time. Maybe you've lived free from the effects of some of those sins, but you are seeing the cycle repeated in your children. It is going to take more than a flyswatter to wipe out an infestation of Beelzebub's minions.

Throughout the Bible, the number 40 represents cleansing and purifying. The flood in Noah's time cleansed the earth of wickedness over 40 days. Moses' life could be divided up into three different seasons of 40: He spent 40 years in Egypt, 40 years in the desert, and 40 years delivering and bringing the people of God to the Promised Land. He also fasted for 40 days on two occasions, once receiving the Laws of God in the form of the Ten Commandments, and the second time, interceding for the sin of the people.

When Jonah was sent to Nineveh, he gave the inhabitants of that city 40 days to repent or expect judgment. The Bible records, "So the people of Nineveh believed God, proclaimed a fast, and put on sackcloth, from the greatest to the least of them." The King called for the entire land to fast saying, "Let neither man nor beast, herd nor flock, taste anything; do not let them eat, or drink water. But let man and beast be covered with sackcloth, and cry mightily to God; yes, let every one turn from his evil way and from the violence that is in his hands. Who can tell if God will turn and relent, and turn away from His fierce anger, so that we may not perish?" Their humility, repentance, and worship was seen by God, and they were rewarded with mercy instead of judgment. (See Jonah 3).

After defeating 450 prophets of Baal and ordering their execution, Elijah fled to the desert to escape the deadly threats of Jezebel. God sent an angel to feed him and watch over him as he rested. When he had eaten the meal the angel prepared for him, he went the next 40 days without food. During that time, he spoke with God and received new direction. His insecurities and doubts were removed, and the oppression of the enemy was broken.

But there's more. The word Elijah received during that 40-day fast even affected the next generation. He followed God's instruction to anoint Jehu, Elisha, and others to finish the work, and Jehu is credited with the utter destruction of the woman Jezebel. As the account goes, those who went to bury her body after she was thrown from the tower found only her skull, her feet, and the palms of her hands. They reported to Jehu, "This is the word of the LORD, which He spoke by His servant Elijah the Tishbite, saying, 'On the plot of ground at Jezreel dogs shall eat the flesh of Jezebel; and the corpse of Jezebel shall be as refuse on the surface of the field, in the plot at Jezreel, so that they shall not say, Here lies Jezebel" (2 Kings 9:36, 37 NKJV).

> THERE IS a prophetic release that occurs in a church or an individual that fasts continually for 40 days.

There is a prophetic release that occurs in a church or an individual who fasts continually for 40 days. The fast does not necessarily have to be from food. What about fasting TV for 40 days, or computer games, or some other time consuming activity that is not productive for the Kingdom? What if you fasted an additional hour of your time each day for 40 days to spend with the Lord? I wonder what kind of cleansing would occur and what kind of glory would be released.

Flies represent demons in the Word, as do other animals. If you could see into the spirit world, many demons resemble animals. For example, the Bible said that when the seed of God's Word is sown, the fowls of the air come to eat it up (see Matt 13:4, 19). When Jesus said, "You will take up serpents" (Mark 16:18), He was referring

> DEVILS WILL START... YOU GUESSED IT... DROPPING LIKE FLIES!

to demon powers. The Bible talks about treading on snakes and scorpions (see Luke 10:19). David, in foretelling Jesus' experience on the cross, said, "The bulls of Bashan have charged me" (Ps 22:12). Those spirits came at Him, goring Him like bulls.

These demon spirits attach themselves to our lives as generational curses, bondages, strongholds of the mind, lust, perversion, addictions of every kind. The problem with most churches is that we just swat at the flies for a few days when they are right up in our faces. They go away for a while, but they keep coming back. It's time to clean house! It's time for a scriptural season of cleansing. Devils will start...you guessed it...dropping like flies! And not only in your life, in your generation, but also the future generation of demons that would be passed down to your children.

Solomon wrote, "Dead flies putrefy the perfumer's ointment, and cause it to give off a foul odor" (Eccl 10:1 NKJV). Flies would get into the special anointing oil, they'd get stuck in it, die, and spoil the fragrance. Flies hinder the anointing in your life. Your worship gets polluted by flies of lust and perversion. We are supposed to walk in that pure anointing that pierces hearts, breaks yokes, delivers from bondages, heals the sick. It's time to get rid of the "flies" in your business, your marriage, your mind, your house. They cannot stand the power of the Holy Ghost and the intimacy of the presence of Jesus that comes from 40 days of bombarding heaven.

Some might say, "But 40 days is a long time!" Is it really? I read an article in our local paper about the Muslim celebration of Ramadan, when all Muslims, old, young, even children, fast from sun-up to sun-down for 30 days. At the end of each of those days, they all come together to break the fast and pray to their god, Allah. It is a form of worship for them, helping them focus on spiritual things instead of earthly needs. They come together all over the world for this 30-day religious event, sacrificing and praying to a god who isn't even alive; his bones are still in the grave. Did you know that Islam is the fastest growing religion in the United States? It is anticipated that in a few years, one-in-four will be converted to Islam.

The scandals and corruption on the front pages of our newspapers and the gross perversion that is prevalent on every level of society tell us how much we need revival in this country. How much more should we, as Christians, devote ourselves to fasting and prayer? God promised, "If My people who are called by My name will humble themselves, and pray and seek My face, and turn from their wicked ways, then I will hear from heaven, and will forgive their sin and heal their land" (2 Chronicles 7:14 NKJV). God does not lie. His promises are true, His rewards are waiting to be released, so what are we waiting for? It

HIS REWARDS ARE WAITING TO BE RELEASED, SO WHAT ARE WE WAITING FOR?

doesn't matter how dark the hour is, or what is going on in the White House, or overseas. God rules and reigns above all those things.

Look at Daniel's fast. For three weeks he said he "ate no pleasant bread" (Dan 10:3). Generally, "pleasant bread" there is thought to mean more festive foods such as sweets and the like. That may not sound like much of a sacrifice until you think about the fact that we're addicted to sugar! According to Dr. Colbert's research, Americans consume roughly 11,250 pounds of sugar in a lifetime! [[Don Colbert, M.D., *Toxic Relief*, (Lake Mary, FL: Siloam Press, 2003), 30.]] If you fasted from just sweets for 40 days, you would rid your body of many toxins and probably shed several pounds. For some of you, it would be a major sacrifice!

> Can you forego that Snickers bar in the afternoon to be delivered from a recurring sin?

Daniel also drank no wine. As a believer in this day and time, that certainly should not be a problem. But then he said he ate no flesh, or meat. That is going to hit a lot of folks hard!

No soft drinks, candy bars, cookies, cakes, sugar-coated cereals (yes, sugar is everywhere in our American diet), no hotdogs, burgers, steaks, beef tacos, barbequed ribs, ham biscuits…I could go on and on.

But God sees that sacrifice. When you go out with people at the office to a steakhouse, and you choose to have the garden salad, baked potato (no bacon-bits), and ice-water instead of that medium-well-done 24-ounce T-bone steak, God takes notice. You're cleansing, you're purifying, and you're destroying flies!

Can you forego that Snickers Bar in the afternoon to be delivered from a recurring sin? To have more of the presence of Jesus in your life, can you drink water instead of sugary, caffeinated drinks for 40 days? Do you want to do more than just swat at those flies of doubt and confusion that inundate your thoughts?

Like Jesus told the disciples at the well in Samaria, when you open yourself to know the will of the Father, and do the will of the Father, no steak compares…no cake compares… nothing can fill you and satisfy you like that. Get ready for the presence of Jesus like you have never had before.

CHAPTER 6

GOD'S
COMING TO DINNER?

"If I were hungry, I would not tell you;

For the world is Mine, and all its fullness.

Will I eat the flesh of bulls,

or drink the blood of goats?

Offer to God thanksgiving,

And pay your vows to the Most High.

Call upon Me in the day of trouble;

I will deliver you, and you shall glorify Me."

—GOD [PSALM 50:12-15 NKJV]

If we are not careful, we can allow life to get us into the same old ruts and routines without even realizing it. Our relationships with the Lord can suffer the same fate. When we don't do what it takes to stay sharp and sensitive to the Holy Spirit, our praise, worship, offerings, and even preaching can become heartless routines to God. As a believer, you can pray, read your Bible, and go to church week after week, and still be losing site of your first love. It is not that you don't love the Lord, but the business of life can bring you to the point of losing your freshness, your enthusiasm, and your sensitivity to His Spirit and what pleases Him.

My mother was an excellent cook. But if she had gotten so caught up in other things that all she ever put on the table for us was meatloaf every night of the week, I don't think it would have taken long for me to find somewhere else to eat. The disappointed sound of comments like, "Aw Mom, meatloaf again?" would have been common at my house. What if God were hungry and all we have to feed Him is our same droll, religious routines day after day? Just like ending up with

I can just hear our heavenly Father sighing, "Religion again?"

meatloaf on the table every night, I can just hear our Heavenly Father sighing, "Religion again?"

That's why God said to Israel, "If I were hungry, I would not tell you; for the world is Mine, and all its fullness" (Psalm 50:12 NKJV). God owns the cattle on a thousand hills. He does not need our routines. He does not savor heartless activity. He does not want our "leftovers" when He can get "fed" elsewhere. True worship that comes from our hearts feeds Him and satisfies Him; it is something He desires—and deserves. Our religiosity of "going through the motions" once a week does not please Him as much as our obedience to His Word.

FASTING IS a CONSTANT MEANS OF RENEWING YOURSELF SPIRITUALLY.

The reason this subject fits in a book about fasting is simple: Fasting is a constant means of renewing yourself spiritually. The discipline of fasting breaks you out of the world's routine. It is a form of worship—offering your body to God as a living sacrifice is holy and pleasing to God (see Romans 12:1). The discipline of fasting will humble you, remind you of your dependency on God, and bring you back to your first love. It causes the roots of your relationship with Jesus to go deeper.

God desires to move powerfully in your life. His plans for you are always progressing and developing. He desires to speak to you, like one would speak to a friend. That's how he spoke with Abraham. When God came to judge the wickedness of Sodom and Gomorrah, He stopped by Abraham's tent on the way. Can you imagine looking outside one day and seeing the Lord walking up to your front door with two angels? Talk about out of the ordinary! Abraham rushed to meet the Lord and bowed low to worship Him. He asked the three visitors to tarry so he could bring water to wash their feet and prepare a meal. The three welcomed his invitation and stayed.

Abraham was a man who worshiped God, who spoke with God, and who had followed God's call to leave everything and follow Him to a land that He would show him. His worship and faithfulness had fed God for many years and suddenly he had the opportunity to feed Him in the natural sense. When you feed God, He will tell you things that He may hide from others. The Bible says that after they ate, God told Abraham he and Sarah would have a son in a year. He even shared with Abraham His plans for Sodom and Gomorrah. Notice, too, that Abraham was then in a very intimate place with God in which he could intercede on behalf of the righteous who

Jentezen Franklin

might be found in those wicked cities.

There are dimensions of our glorious King that will never be revealed to the casual, disinterested worshiper. There are walls of intercession that will never be scaled by dispassionate religious service. But when you take steps to break out of the ordinary and worship Him as He deserves, you will begin to see facets of His being you never knew existed. He will begin to share secrets with you about Himself, His plans, His desires for you. When you worship God as He deserves, He is magnified.

David was a man after God's heart. He was a man who fasted often, and not just from food. As a youth, he was often in the fields alone with just the sheep and his God. After he was anointed king, he spent many days running for his life. David wrote Psalm 34 while alone and on the run from Saul in the land of the Philistines. But David stirred himself to worship God even in those conditions, proclaiming, "His praise shall continually be in my mouth," and "Taste and see that the Lord is good." A routine worshiper in those circumstances would have been totally overwhelmed. But David knew that to worship God was to magnify God. His invitation to all of us to "Magnify the LORD with me," still stands open today.

When I was a kid, we didn't have toys like Play Station and Nintendo. We just had real simple toys and great imaginations. One of the best gifts my parents ever gave me was a big, hand-held magnifying glass. To a six or seven-year old boy, a magnifying glass is adventure waiting to happen! If I lined it up just right with the light of the sun I could concentrate the heat from that light and burn a hole in a piece of trash, or even toast an unsuspecting ant. And of course, there was the main feature: the ability to enlarge anything you wanted to look at. When I held that glass up to an object, I could see aspects of it that couldn't possibly be seen with normal vision. Magnification didn't make that object any bigger than it actually was, but it greatly enlarged my view, allowing me to see details that were hidden without magnification.

David was calling us to worship the Lord with Him. When you worship, you magnify God. Your enemies or circumstances may seem to be so large and so powerful that they are all you can see.

WHEN YOU WORSHIP, YOU MAGNIFY GOD.

But when you worship, you not only magnify God, but you also reduce the size and power of everything else around you. Later in Psalm 34, David said, "I sought the LORD, and He heard me, and delivered me from all my fears." God will hear you when you set your heart to worship Him. When you magnify the Lord, you shrink the supposed power of your enemy, the devil. The greatest thing you can do in the midst of a battle is to magnify the Lord. Jehoshaphat is proof of that. When under attack, the whole nation cried out, fasted, and worshipped God. Jehoshaphat sent the praisers out ahead of the army to magnify their God, and He utterly delivered Judah from their enemy.

When Jesus spoke with the woman at the well in Samaria, His words set her free. She had been married many times and was living with a man who was not her husband. Her relatives had routinely worshiped in Samaria, but had been told they were to worship in Jerusalem. At Jacob's well, Jesus taught her that the "true worshipers will worship the Father in spirit and truth; for the Father is seeking such to worship Him." With everything else He said to her, she knew she had found the Messiah, or at least, He had found her. So she ran back to town, telling everyone, "Come see a Man who told me all things that I ever did." The Bible says the town came out to see and hear Him—to worship Him.

In the meantime, His disciples returned with food, but He told them He was not hungry. He said, "I have food to eat of which you do not know...My food is to do the will of Him who sent Me, and to finish His work." (See John 4:6-34.) The worship of that woman had so satisfied Jesus that He was no longer hungry for natural food. The disciples were busy gathering food, but she took time to worship and feed Him that which He most desired.

What is God saying about you? Is it, "Religion again?" Or does He dine with you, fellowship with you, and share with you deep secrets and plans for the future? Whatever you may be facing or going through right now, I want you to heed David's call to "magnify the Lord." If you are in a rut or a routine where your worship just isn't cutting it...if you have not heard God speak to you in a long time...if your circumstances seem to be the biggest obstacle in your life..., stop everything and begin a fast. One day, several days, some food, all food—the details are not as important as your heart's desire to satisfy God with your worship and sacrifice.

CHAPTER 7

YOU SHALL BE FILLED

It is written,
Man shall not live by bread alone,
but by every word that proceedeth
out of the mouth of God.
—JESUS [MATTHEW 4:4]

Our American diets are loaded with sugars, toxins, processed foods, meats, etc. Yet it is possible for us to be eating large meals, be overweight, and STILL be malnourished. In Colbert's book, *Toxic Relief*, he states, "We may be actually starving from a nutritional standpoint, while at the same time becoming grossly obese…Sadly, we really are digging our graves with our forks and knives!" [[p 32]]

In that sense, it is easy to see how our physical lives again parallel our spiritual lives. We can become "overnourished" on a hefty diet of church programs and activities, religious structure and traditions of men, and yet be severely undernourished when it comes to the deeper things of God. Do you know what Dr. Colbert refers to as the "single most effective answer to overnourishment"? Fasting. He has found that "more than anything else, fasting is the dynamic key to cleansing your body from a lifetime collection of toxins, reversing overnourishment and the diseases it brings and ensuring a wonderful future of renewed energy, vitality, longevity, and blessed health." [[p 39]]

WHEN YOU HUNGER FOR GOD, HE WILL FILL YOU.

Jesus said, "Blessed are those who hunger and thirst for righteousness, for they shall be filled" (Matt 5:6). When you begin to develop a hunger for the deeper things of God, He will fill you. However, sometimes just being in a good service is not enough. I believe God is already raising up people in this hour who do not want a diet of just "church as normal" any longer. I see it at Free Chapel; people are fasting, and developing a hunger for more of God and religious traditions are having to just get out of the way. Hungry people are desperate people. They will push over the custom, they will push over the ritual—they don't want to leave hungry.

Jesus found such hunger while visiting Tyre and Sidon. A woman whose daughter was possessed and tormented by a devil heard that He was there. But the woman was Greek, "a Syro-Phoenician by birth," and, therefore, outside of the covenant God had made with Israel. But that didn't matter to her. She was hungry and her faith was persistent. Even when Jesus discouraged her saying that the "bread" was first for the children of Israel, she was hungry enough to ask for even a crumb that would fall to the floor. Many of the "children who sat at the table" had not shown such great hunger. Jesus honored her request and her daughter was healed because of her persistence (see Mark 7:25-30).

Hungry people are desperate people and they are hungry for more of God than they have ever had. They are breaking out of religious rules, regulations, and traditional thinking and breaking through to more of His Presence…more of His power to turn situations around…more of His healing power… more of His miracle-working power! Only Jesus satisfies that hunger!

WHEN YOU HUNGER FOR MORE, YOU WILL RECEIVE MORE.

It was just such hunger that was stirred in the heart of a Gentile centurion in Caesarea who fasted, prayed to God always, and gave generously to the poor. Though they were Gentiles, Cornelius and his household devoutly feared and served God. As Cornelius was fasting and praying one day, like Daniel, an angel appeared to him with a message. The angel said, "Your prayers and your alms have come up for a memorial before God." And then the angel instructed him to send for Peter, who was nearby in Joppa. Peter, who was fasting at the time as well, saw a vision from God in which many foods that were unlawful for Jews to eat were presented to him. He was still puzzled by the vision when Cornelius' messengers arrived. Going with them to his house the next day and hearing of the hunger in this man's heart, Peter understood that the vision meant that the Gospel was not to be withheld from the Gentiles. As he shared the

Gospel with those of Cornelius' household, the Holy Spirit fell and baptized them all, and later they were baptized in water (see Acts 10).

Fasting stirs a hunger in your spirit that goes deeper than the temporary hunger you experience in your flesh. When you hunger for God, He will fill you. Jesus went through cities where He could do no miracles—because there was no hunger. As Jesus entered Capernaum, He was confronted by a Roman centurion whose servant was paralyzed and tormented (see Matthew 8:5-13). But the centurion knew it would take only a word from Jesus for the servant to be healed. When he said those words to Jesus, the Bible says He was amazed at his faith and told those around Him, "I have not found such great faith, not even in Israel!" He was saying, "So many in Abraham's lineage don't have the hunger this man has shown. They come to see Me but they don't hunger." In this day, God is saying, "I'm looking for somebody who wants something, I'm looking for somebody who will do more than show up, but they will hunger for that which I want to place into them!"

God honors what others call "unlawful" hunger. Matthew 12:1-8 tells of a time when Jesus and the disciples were walking and talking together. The disciples became hungry, and as they walked they "began to pluck heads of grain and to eat."

But it was unlawful to "pick grain" on the day of rest. That day you were not to labor for yourself but be devoted to the Lord. So when the Pharisees noticed what the disciples were doing, they said, "Your disciples are doing what is not lawful to do on the Sabbath!" But they were walking and talking with the Lord of the Sabbath! So Jesus said to the Pharisees, "Have you not read what David did when he was hungry, he and those who were with him: how he entered the house of God and ate the showbread which was not lawful for him to eat, nor for those who were with him, but only for the priests? Yet I say to you that in this place there is One greater than the temple. But if you had known what this means, 'I desire mercy and not sacrifice,' you would not have condemned the guiltless. For the Son of Man is Lord even of the Sabbath" (NKJV).

The Pharisees couldn't move past their own traditions to recognize that the Bread of Life stood before them. They were satisfied with their own religion and did not hunger. But when you hunger for more, you will receive more. God will break all the religious rules for you. Perhaps someone has told you, "With your background, God can't use you." Or, "Because you're a woman, you can't preach." Or, "You don't have the right 'connections' to do what you want to do." When you hunger for God, He will break the rules of man and cause His favor to come on your life.

Anybody can be normal. Someone has to say, "But I want more! LORD, I'm hungry! I'm going to have to push tradition aside! I'm going to have to push religious rules aside! I'm going to have to push all of the rituals aside because I'm starving to death and I just can't make it on church-as-usual any longer." My suggestion is to begin by pushing the plate aside. Show God that you are serious. We must get to the place where we are desperate for God again. We must begin to desire Him more than food or drink. Let us be filled with the Bread of Presence instead of the refuse of religion. Begin to make fasting a regular discipline and see how God answers your hunger!

CHAPTER 8

REWARDED OPENLY

Do not be afraid, Abram. I am your shield,

your exceedingly great reward.

—GOD [GENESIS 15:1 NKJV]

G od said, "Let the priests, who minister to the LORD, weep between the porch and the altar." (Joel 2:17 NKJV). On a house, the "porch" is the part everybody can see; it represents the more public aspects of your ministry. The altar represents private ministry. In the life of a believer, there should always be more private than public ministry to God. When you read about Jesus, you do not see Him praying in public nearly as much as you see Him praying in private. The Bible says He would often pray through the night; intimate times alone with His Father. Out of those times in private devotion, public demonstrations of God's power would be poured forth in healings, raising the dead, abundance, and more. Victories are not won in public, but in private. That is why fasting, whether corporately or individually, is a private discipline. Where there is little private discipline, there is little public reward.

Earlier I showed you how in Matthew chapter 6, Jesus detailed the three duties of a Christian: giving, praying, and fasting. There is something else I want you to see in that chapter. Jesus said, "Take heed that you do not do your charitable deeds before men, to be seen by them. Otherwise you have no reward from your Father in Heaven." He was talking about public and private ministry. He added, "When you do a charitable deed, do not sound a trumpet before you as the hypocrites do in the synagogues and in the streets, that they may have glory from men. Assuredly, I say to you, they have their reward. But when you do a charitable deed, do not let your left hand know what your right hand is doing, that your charitable deed may be in secret; and your Father who sees in secret will Himself reward you openly" (Matt 6:1-4 NKJV).

Whether done corporately or individually, fasting is a personal, private discipline. It is a sacrifice born out of expectancy. That is not to imply that fasting is a manipulative tool to get something from God, but a "reasonable act of service" (Romans 12:1), that God rewards openly. Remember the hundred fold return? God's rewards are for all to see. Just look at the life of Job. He went through a devastating trial and lost everything. His wealth, his family and his health were all stripped away. Yet he prayed, he fasted, and he remained faithful to private devotion. Job said, "I have esteemed the words of His mouth more than my necessary food" (Job 23:12). And God "restored Job's losses," and gave him "twice as much as he

FASTING WILL BREAK POVERTY OFF YOUR LIFE.

had before." The Bible also says that He "blessed the latter days of Job more than the first," and even gave him more sons and daughters. God's open rewards flooded Job's life.

Now I want to share with you some of the open rewards that God told me He would pour out on us at Free Chapel as we were diligent to seek Him in giving, praying, and fasting. These same rewards are open to every believer!

First, He told me that fasting will break poverty off your life. As I plant a seed each time I fast, major blessings return on my life. Again looking at Joel (2:15-16), the people were so poor and in such a famine that they couldn't even bring an offering. But God said to, "Blow the trumpet in Zion, sanctify a fast, call a solemn assembly." After that fast, the threshing floor was full of wheat, the oil vats were overflowing, and they ate in plenty and were satisfied. The Lord brought great financial blessing to people who fasted and prayed. When fasting is a lifestyle, poverty will not be.

> HEALTH AND HEALING WILL FOLLOW FASTING.

That does not mean that you can fast soft drinks for one day and fall into wealth. But if you begin to fast on a regular basis, and you begin to honor God with fasting, prayer, and giving, you will see for yourself that it is directly linked to prosperity and poverty coming off your life. It is interesting that the three wisest men in the Old Testament, Joseph, Daniel, and Solomon, were also the three wealthiest men! Joseph was forced to fast in prison. According to history, only the prisoner's family members were allowed to bring them food, and his family was in another country. But after that season of his life, Joseph became fabulously wealthy and was put over all the money of Egypt (see Genesis 41:39-45). Solomon humbled himself in fasting and in prayer and God greatly increased his wealth and wisdom (see 1 Kings 3:10-13). Likewise, Daniel, who diligently sought God through fasting and prayer while in Babylonian captivity, was given wisdom over all the others and greatly prospered in the days of Darius the king (see Daniel 6:1-4).

God also said that health and healing would follow fasting. Of His chosen fast God said, "Then your light shall break forth like the morning, your healing shall spring forth speedily"(Isaiah 58:8 NKJV). Fasting humbles you and brings clarity, even allowing you to get unforgiveness and bitterness out of your heart. Some people have tried and tried to truly forgive someone, but have never been able to let the matter go. Begin a fast and trust God to work that in your heart. Earlier in the book, I told you how fasting helps you physically because it cleanses your body and gives your organs time to rest. It also helps you "spring clean" in a spiritual sense, because it makes you sensitive to the desires of the Lord. Unforgiveness, bitterness, and the like can all be linked to illnesses, fatigue, stress, and more.

Fasting will also overcome sexual addictions and demonic powers.

When we've been preparing for our annual fasts, the Lord has told me to hold miracle services. He said, "I want you to take a half or full-page ad in the paper. Tell those who are diseased, suffering with AIDS, leukemia, heart disease…that there is a church that has been fasting and seeking God for healing." When you fast and pray, you should EXPECT miracles to follow.

Fasting will also overcome sexual addictions and demonic powers. It will break great sin off people. In Matthew 17:21, Jesus said of that stubborn demon that "this kind comes out only with fasting and prayer," remember? There's a phenomenal story in the book of Judges, chapters 19 and 20, where fasting made the difference in a major battle against a people overcome with sexual perversion. A Levite was traveling with his concubine and stopped in the land of Gibeah, which belonged to the Benjamites. The men of that city had become wicked and delighted in lewd homosexual acts (Judges 19:22).

The men surrounded the house the Levite was visiting and demanded that he be sent out so they could "know him carnally." They ended up brutally raping and murdering the man's concubine instead and she died on the doorstep of the house. When he found her lying there the next morning, he was outraged. He sent pieces of her body with a word to all the tribes of Israel, condemning them for allowing that sort of wickedness to exist in their midst and demanding that they rise-up and do something about it.

The armies of Israel gathered against Benjamin. They went out to fight and lost 22,000 men the first day (Judges 20:21). They came back, regrouped, and fought against the Benjamites again, this time losing 18,000 (Judges 20:25). Before they went out to fight the third day, God sent the prophet Phinehas with a message to FAST and pray. So the men fasted for twenty-four hours and when they went back out against that homosexual spirit, its power was broken and it was defeated (see Judges 20:26-48)!

Now we don't wrestle with flesh and blood. But there is a spirit behind homosexuality. There is a spirit behind pornography. There is a spirit behind adultery. There is a spirit behind fornication. These demonic spirits of perversion manipulate and use people like puppets on a string. But fasting will break the stronghold of demonic sexual addictions like pornography, homosexuality, adultery, fornication, and lust.

GOD WILL ALSO TARGET YOUR CHILDREN.

God will also target your children who are being led off and destroyed by the enemy's devices. In the book of Joel, God called for a holy fast. And He said, "It shall come to pass afterward that I will pour out My Spirit on all flesh; your sons and your daughters shall prophesy..." (Joel 2:28 NKJV). Many times the rewards of fasting come "after" the fast, though from time to time answers can come during the fast. Look at the story of Hezekiah's son, Manasseh, who became king of Judah (see 2 Chron 33:1-13). Manasseh was a wicked king whom God had warned many times to no avail. Then the army of Assyria captured Hezekiah's son, put a hook in his nose, bound him in chains and took him to Babylon. In his distress, Manasseh cried out to God, and humbled himself with fasting. The Bible says God heard his plea and "brought him back to Jerusalem into his kingdom...and Manasseh knew that the Lord is God."

I have heard so many stories of children who were backslidden and being drawn away by the enemy. As with a hook in their nose, they wind up bound to pornography, trapped by drugs, alcohol, and every sort of addiction. Maybe you have rebellious children, or sons and daughters who are committing fornication, but I'm telling you, fasting and praying will absolutely break those spirits off their lives.

I received this letter from Vickie, a member of our congregation, about her son. She writes:

"My son was a born-again, Holy Ghost-filled, fifteen-year-old when his dad committed suicide. He turned his back on God and ran from Him for the past fifteen years, but God never gave up on him! He and his brand-new wife came to service after their wedding in Tennessee. They sat in the balcony. When you gave the altar call, you wouldn't give up. You said, "The Holy Spirit won't let me stop. He says there is someone here that if you don't take this opportunity today, you will never get another one." My son said he looked up and you were pointing right at him. He looked over at his new wife and said, "Well, are we going?" Both

of them came down and accepted Jesus as their Lord and Savior. His new wife was raised Buddhist and had never heard about Jesus until she met my son. Thank you for not letting "time" get in the way of one more salvation! My fast ended January 22, and 10 days later two of my requests were answered!"

"I will reward you openly." God does not lie. He has spoken to me that He will bring in souls during our annual fasts and we have seen the fruit of that reward as well. The thirty, sixty, and hundred-fold returns are available in the life of every believer. God is no respecter of persons...what He has done in our church, in the lives of our members, He will do for you when you set your heart to seek Him through fasting.

CHAPTER 9

NOTHING SHALL BE IMPOSSIBLE— IT WORKS!

I will praise the name of God with a song,

And will magnify Him with thanksgiving.

This also shall please the LORD

better than an ox or bull,

Which has horns and hooves.

The humble shall see this and be glad;

And you who seek God,

your hearts shall live.

—KING DAVID [PSALM 69:30-32 NKJV]

I could tell you more and more of what God will do when you fast, but the testimonies of people from Free Chapel who participate in our yearly fast say it all. My heart is overwhelmed every year when we begin hearing the testimonies of healings, financial blessings, lost children being brought home, and more.

Take Janine's story for example. She had worked at Dupont for fifteen years, but lost her job when they were bought out by Bristol Myers. Making matters more overwhelming, in December, Janine's 35-year-old brother died suddenly, leaving her deeply grieved and broken hearted. She found the grace to join the fast with the church at the beginning of the year. To her amazement, Bristol Myers contacted her in March and said, "We're going to give you a year's salary and extended benefits for a full year." With that money, she and her husband became debt free, except for their home, and were able to purchase a newer vehicle. She later told us that, as a result of the fast, God had restored her desire to live.

Isaac and his wife, Darrence, were told that they could not have any children. They went on the 21-day fast. Later that year he testified, "The devil tried to destroy the Lord's blessing, but we have a baby in our arms this year that we didn't have this time last year!"

I received a note from Joida, another of our members, who wrote, "My husband took the challenge of the 21-day fast, even though he was not yet saved. Fourteen days into the fast, he woke up in the middle of the night crying. The next morning he gave his life to Christ, and was baptized in the Holy Ghost that night! Not only did my husband get saved on a 21-day fast, but on February 13, my husband and all of our children, even my sister-in-law, were baptized. To God be the glory!"

Laura and her son, Drake, also attend Free Chapel. Life came to a jolting halt for them at one point after Drake was diagnosed with leukemia. He had gone through chemotherapy and had all the side-effects. On January 5, the first Sunday in January when we began the fast, Drake was lying in the Intensive Care Unit, literally fighting for his life with a 107-degree fever. I knew the severity of the situation, so I proclaimed that we would begin that fast for Drake's recovery. Laura told me Drake awoke at that same moment—the fever broke, he suffered no brain damage, and the leukemia went into total remission.

But Laura's story doesn't stop there. She joined the 21-day fast that year and continued on it for a full 40 days.

This mother, in financial crisis, with a son near death and suffering from leukemia, fasted for 40 days. God honors that kind of faith and devotion. The Holy Spirit spoke to a man and his wife in our church to buy Laura a brand new van. I called her and asked if she could come by the church office, but didn't tell her anything further. On her way, the car she was driving at the time broke down! She finally arrived, terribly apologetic, having no idea what was about to happen. I handed her the keys to a beautiful new van complete with a DVD player for Drake to enjoy—and a check for an extra $5000 the couple wanted her to have!

Several weeks later, I called her up on the platform and we shared her testimony. Earlier that morning, I asked her how much debt she was in. She said she only owed $20,000 on her house, because she had paid off all her other debts with the prior $5000 gift. In that morning service, I presented her with another check from that same couple, this time for $25,000. Laura and her son lived their last year in poverty, thanks to the open reward that God poured out on their sacrificial obedience.

One year, only three days into the fast, Sharon testified that her father, who had been battling prostate cancer, was suddenly and miraculously healed. The doctors went in to do a procedure and, to their shock, could find no signs of the cancer anywhere! She began the fast on his behalf and God healed him. What I loved about her testimony was that she did not stop after the three days. She said, "I'm going longer to see what else God wants to do." God is no respecter of persons. His delight is to reward His children. He is honored and magnified when we are willing to seek Him at all costs.

Fasting will bring your life and your ministry to others out of obscurity. One Sunday, Harry testified that he had gone on to fast the full 40 days. He said:

> *"I've got a ministry called Walk on Water Ministries. I go into prisons and jails full-time. But I'll be honest with you, I'm a preacher and I'm filled with the Holy Spirit, but God told me I had a spirit of gluttony on me. That is why I began this fast. I didn't ask for God to open doors, I told God I was sick of the spirit of gluttony cheating me out of the spiritual things God had for my life and locking doors and locking finances and locking everything else that God has for me."*

This brother started seeing more doors open for him than he could even handle. He began getting invitations to share at other prisons, to be interviewed by TV Stations — he was even interviewed by a policeman who used to arrest him before Harry gave his life to the Lord.

On the 12th day of the fast one year, Jack testified that his older brother had been diagnosed with hepatitis and was dying. The doctors said there was no hope. His liver was totally shut down. He was taking $700 shots every week that made him even sicker for three days after. Since he owns his own business, he lost a lot of work. But he didn't want to take the shots on the weekends because he didn't want to lose time with his family. Worst of all, Jack's brother was unsaved. Jack and his wife began the fast praying that, even though his brother was unsaved, God would heal him. Only a few days into the fast, they learned that the brother had gone to the doctor and not a trace of hepatitis could be found in his body!

The Lord has assured me over the years that fasting will bring in the lost. Mary told us about her 29-year-old unsaved cousin, Joy, who called her out of the blue during the annual fast. She was troubled, and wanted to get together with Mary, saying, "We don't have to eat or anything. I just need to talk with you." Joy began to share with Mary about problems she was having with her marriage and more. Mary told her, "The best thing you can do, Joy, is to find a relationship with Jesus for yourself. I don't know if you've ever prayed or accepted Him, but I can't leave here today without asking if you have ever been saved." Joy willingly prayed with her cousin and accepted Christ for the first time in her life!

Fasting makes you more sensitive to the timing and voice of the Holy Spirit. Even in the middle of the fast, Mary had a boldness that she typically might not have had. Fasting does such a work in your life that the lost are often drawn to you and to what God is doing. It's not that we manipulate God through our "works," forcing His hand. Fasting simply breaks you and brings your faith to a new level.

By this point, I hope that I have been able to clear up the misconceptions about what fasting is, and what it is not—and why it is a discipline that should not be missing in the life of any believer. It is a vital part of that threefold cord of normal Christian duties that Jesus outlined in Matthew 6 — giving, praying, and fasting. It cleanses your body and promotes health in many practical ways. It brings you into a deeper relationship with the Lord than can be enjoyed through routine religion. Don't wait for a good time, as God pointed out—there just isn't one. You are not too young or too old. After all, Anna was a prophetess who was in her

80's when she worshiped day and night, fasting and praying (see Luke 2:37).

As I mentioned earlier, if Jesus could have received what He needed to walk out His ministry here on earth—without fasting—He would not have fasted. But He did fast; in fact, He has continued fasting for us for over 2000 years. During His last meal with the disciples, He gave them the cup and said, "I will not drink of this fruit of the vine from now on until that day when I drink it new with you in My Father's kingdom" (Matt 26:29-30 NKJV). I have seen people who have never fasted before experience marvelous breakthroughs in their lives. If you are ready to bring supernatural blessings into your life and release the power of God to overcome any situation, begin today making the discipline of fasting a part of your life. You will be greatly rewarded!

notes

notes

notes

notes

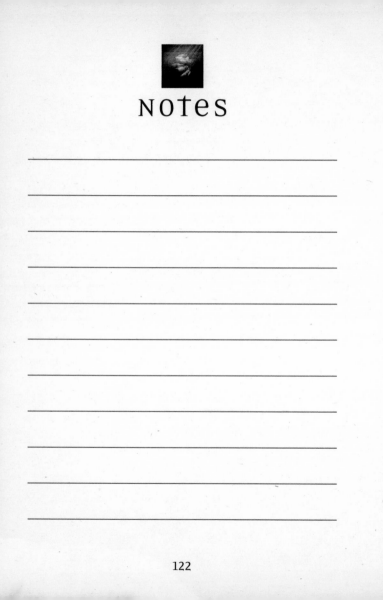

Notes

notes

ABOUT THE AUTHOR

J entezen Franklin pastors a thriving congregation at Free Chapel in Gainesville, Georgia. A gifted musician and singer, he is driven by a passion for bringing people into the presence of God through anointed preaching and teaching. Television broadcasts of his *Kingdom Connection* programs can be seen across the country and beyond, and have caused him to be a much in-demand speaker. He and his wife Cherise make their home in Georgia with their five children.

KEEP YOUR
UNDERWEAR ON
(Available on video or DVD)